Happy God's Way

Donnadene King

Hoot Books Publishing LLC
Abingdon, VA
copyright © 2025 Donnadene King
ISBN: 978-1-959700-55-5

Dedication

To my beautiful Mother, Joann New, the smartest woman I know. You have inspired me to enjoy every single day- the good and the *not so good*. Your childlike faith in God, and joy in the midst of trying times, is an inspiration to many, and to mis-quote my pastor Jarrod- "You are one tough ole bird." You are indeed an inspiration to me and countless others.

Table of Contents

Foreword

"My heart is inditing a good matter.
I speak of the things which I have made
touching the king: my tongue is the pen
of a ready writer." (Psalms 45:1; KJV)

. . ."Go in peace; the journey on which
you are going is acceptable to the Lord."
(Judges 18:6; AMP)

Sitting on my front porch, coffee and prayer; enjoying the warm fall evening; suddenly this verse was illuminated in my heart. I had never seen this version before...**"your journey is acceptable to the Lord."** All throughout the evening I continually thought on that verse; *God approves our journey.* I thought about my hopes, and dreams- to write an inspirational book. I knew the thought and desire was in my heart; indeed, I had written for years. However, I had never published, or really sought to do so.

The next day, during a menial task, a thought dropped in my heart- *go ahead and write your book; your journey has been approved, by God*. Tears, as I knew at that moment, it was time. I was to move forward in the monumental task of *putting it all together*, publishing years of writing- it was indeed time- what joy!

Looking back, I recall God impressing on my heart, years ago, that He had good plans for me. I felt He was calling me to a specific task. I had always had talents and desires in the areas of motivational speaking and writing. Through the years I had been blessed, some, to use my talents- teaching Sunday School; speaking in church; publishing an article through our local college- but this call was bigger somehow. I knew God was calling me to a higher platform.

It was time to move. I started with prayer. What is your good plan for me, Dear God? How will You use all You have given me? Waiting with a reining ear, I eventually heard; *you will help those who have lost; those who need restoration; you will encourage others; speak and pray.*

The Dream

Walking is something I attempt to do daily, mostly short walks. My walks are about one mile, or more as I don't attempt marathon status. However, in my dream I had walked so very far that it would take me hours to get home. I recall looking at the distance thinking, *I can't do it, it is too far.* I pondered calling someone to come and get me. Instead, I stared out on the long, daunting journey back home. I had only walked a few short minutes when suddenly I realized I was home; impossible! The long, long journey was over in a matter of minutes.

Upon waking, I immediately thought of the huge task before me; the monumental undertaking of writing an entire book. Each chapter needed to be outlined; rough drafts; rewrites; citing sources; locating verses; . . . on and on I reasoned; all the while considering the dream.

What was God showing me? As I thought about the content of the dream, I began to understand that God can propel me in the midst of this huge undertaking. What should take years, God can cause to come together in a short time, a short journey. His Way, His Will, His Timing.

Introduction/Verses

. . . *"grow in grace, and in the knowledge of our Lord and Savior Jesus Christ. To Him be glory both now and forever. Amen."*
(2 Peter 3:18; KJV)

"Come to Me, all you who labour and are heavy laden, and I will give you rest. Take My yoke upon you and learn of Me, for I am gentle and lowly in heart, and you will find rest for your souls."
(Matt.11:28-29; NKJV)

"Now the God of hope fill you with all joy and peace in believing, that ye may abound in hope, through the power of the Holy Ghost." (Romans 15: 13 KJV)

"May the God of hope fill you with all joy and peace in believing (through the experience of your faith) that by the power of the Holy Spirit you will abound in hope and overflow with confidence in His promises." (Romans 15:13 AMP)

"God is our refuge and strength, a very present help in trouble." (Psalms 46:1 NKJV)

Introduction

As an elementary teacher, one of the questions I ask my students is, "Why do writer's write?" Posing that question to myself, I realize that my answer would be, to share my experiences with the reader; to connect with others; to cause the reader to laugh, rejoice, and think about their own circumstances in a different light.

My hope is that the reader would begin to see that God has a very good, specific plan for their lives. Indeed, joy comes when we begin to understand that God walks us through places on purpose to work a wonderful work in us. He is our good shepherd, always leading us to higher ground.

So much of my book, sharing of my own experiences, stems from years of growing seasons in my life.

Seasons that changed me from *glory to glory.* Seasons that changed my perspective; seasons that were hard but that I am eternally grateful to have walked through to the other side.

As you read about my personal experiences, my hope is that you connect to my stories, seasons. That you see your own situation differently through eyes of hope and expectation. That you begin to see that God has a purpose in all He allows, a good plan. That you see, know, and understand the Father's love for you, right where you are.

Corrie Ten Boom describes God's handiwork in our lives like an embroidery, whose threads are *knotted and tangled. However,* that is the underside. When you turn the piece over, you see God's work in your life— a beautiful masterpiece.

Chapter 1

God's Love

"Beloved, if God so loved us, we also ought to love one another."
(I John 4:11 NKJV)

Perched in the choir loft, long maroon robe down to my shoes, *don't trip!* Looking out over the congregation; waiting, pondering, and nervously twisting my index cards; praying, hoping, and listening for that *still small voice.* On and on I prayed, knowing it was the *midnight hour- pastor's address; first song; pastor reads verses; choir sings; and finally, my message. Dear God, one word, just one word to share- suddenly with no time to spare, I heard- Tell them how much you love them- whew! Relief and* joy flooded my heart as I maneuvered my way past choir members, in the little space provided; sweet tears as I

approached the podium, not
tripping on my robe.
Good morning, I began my
message, when I first knew I was
going to speak today, I asked God,
in prayer, if I could purchase a new
outfit. You see I had been walking
through a budget season. God was
teaching me to purchase only those
things that I *really needed;* to stay on
a budget. I reasoned that I really
needed a new outfit if I was to give
a speech before the congregation;
not to mention the public television
audience. The congregation
enjoyed a good belly laugh when I
shared the word I received; *you will
be wearing your choir robe.*
Recovering I added, well I guess that
means no new shoes either.

Looking out over the congregation,
my church family, every familiar face
so precious in my heart. I was
overwhelmed at that moment by
pure love and joy. Finding my voice,
I began to share how very much

they all meant to me; how much I loved them all; how beautiful and precious they were to me. God truly loves me, I continued through tears, to allow me to be a part of this wonderful group.

We are indeed called to love one another, as God loves us. At that moment I experienced that love as never before. Because He loves us, we can love and serve each other. We can bear each other's burdens. We can become a church body, a family through Christ.

God does love us. He longs for us to know His great love; and fulfill His commission to love one another. It is vital that we know and understand just how much He loves us; looks for us, and longs for us. We find rest, hope, and joy when we return to Him with our whole heart, mind, soul, and body.

We see God's love reflected in the story of the prodigal son.

> ➢ And He said, A certain man had two sons:
> ➢ And the younger of them said to *his* father, Father, give me the portion of goods that falleth to me. And he divided unto them *his* living.
> ➢ And not many days after the younger son gathered all together, and took his journey into a far country, and there wasted his substance with riotous living.
> ➢ And when he had spent all, there arose a mighty famine in that land; and he began to be in want.
> ➢ And he went and joined himself to a citizen of that country; and he sent him into his fields to feed swine.
> ➢ And he would have filled his belly with the husk that the

swine did eat: and no man gave unto him.

> And when he came unto himself, he said, how many hired servants of my fathers have bread enough to spare, and I perish with hunger! I will arise and go to my father, and will say to him, Father I have sinned against heaven, and before thee,

> And am no more worthy to be called thy son: make me as one of thy hired servants. (Luke 15: 11-19 KJV)

I love that moment, *when he came to himself;* that pivotal moment of change; of returning, hoping. Not knowing if he would be received but longing just to be a *hired servant.* That moment reminds me of a sweet old song-

>*I will arise and go the Jesus,*
>*He will embrace me in His arms,*
>*In the arms of my dear Savior,*
>*O there are ten thousand charms.*

With the faintest hope, the wayward son picks himself up and begins the long arduous journey home, retracing his steps from years ago. Heavyhearted, weighted with fear and hunger; his joy long gone from his previous journey toward *riotous* living.

Trudging forward, the young son knew his only hope was in his father's mercy. He pushed on with the faintest hope of just being a hired servant. Thoughts of doubt and shame plagued him with every step. Humbled, he reasoned that he would work hard, he would make restitution. Onward he walked, preparing his plea; stumbling in the heat, tears stinging his weathered face; tasting the mire and filth of many wasted years.

But oh, the father's heart, daily looking and longing for his lost son; scanning the horizon with just a glimmer of hope. Many questions troubling his weary soul- Is my son hungry, sick, tired? Have I lost him forever? Weary and tired, the father continues his vigil, perched on his lookout post; expectation waning with each passing day.

And then one day, one glorious day, the father looks out as far as his aged eyes could see- a silhouette- or maybe just a shadow playing tricks on an old man's heart; but still a moment of hope- could it be?; oh glory, could it be? The father didn't dare look away for fear that the image, the hope, might be gone forever. Closer and closer still – No, it is not my imagination, he reasoned, or the heat, for I see my son. I see my long-lost son.

"Quick bring my best robe," the father calls out as he begins to run toward the image, tripping over his own robe. "Hurry," he calls to his servants, "my son who was lost, is found; prepare a great feast."

The father runs faster and faster bridging the gap between them; tears of joy running down his weathered face.

Closer and closer still- finally face to face. His son begins to speak; " just a morsel of your forgiveness," he pleads, "just a crumb from your table." The father begins kissing his filthy face placing his best robe over his tattered clothes, all the while weeping with great joy. "My son, my son who was lost is found, prepare a great feast," he continues to shout with great joy; *and they began to celebrate. (Luke 15:20-24)*

As I read this scene, I am reminded of a verse . . ."for He has clothed me with garments of salvation, He hath covered me with the robe of righteousness . . ."(Isaiah 61:10 KJV)

The Lost Sheep

The father's heart in the parable serves as a reflection of our Heavenly Father's heart for us. He longs for, looks for His lost sheep.

> ➤ And He spake this parable unto them, saying, "What man of you, having a hundred sheep, if he lose one of them, doth not leave the ninety and nine in the wilderness, and go after that which is lost, until he find it?
> ➤ And when he hath found it, he layeth it over his shoulders, rejoicing.
> ➤ And when he cometh home, he calleth together *his* friends and neighbors, saying unto them, "Rejoice with me; for I have found my sheep which was lost.
> ➤ I say unto you, that likewise joy shall be in heaven over one sinner that repenteth, more than over ninety and nine just

persons, which need no repentance. (Luke 15:3-7 KJV)

Our Heavenly Father seeks us out as lost sheep and restores us unto Himself. My sweet mother often says through tears, *"I am so thankful that God took me back into His little fold."*

The Pig Pen

A child of God, a blood bought son or daughter, can choose to stray. They can choose the miserable life of lingering in the pig pen; but oh, what joy when they come to themselves; pick themselves up, and run to their Father's open arms. Their Father who has been looking for, longing for, and waiting for them.

God is, indeed, our Loving Father. He is a God of restoration. He restores unto us more than we lost, *double for our trouble (see Isaiah 61:7).*

We don't have to beg or pay a penance. For God restores us completely- not as a hired servant- but as a son, or daughter. He puts a robe of righteousness on us (see Isaiah 61:10); *and gives us joy for mourning; a garment of praise, for the spirit of heaviness.* (see Isaiah 61:3).

He is a restorer of paths to dwell in; the lifter of our heads; a Loving Father who bids us to, "Come unto Me, all ye who labour and are heavy laden, and I will give you rest." (Matthew 11:28 KJV); also (see Psalms 3:3)

Praise

Praise You, Dear God that You look for us; You long for us. You sent your Son Jesus to die for our sins, that we might be restored unto You. You cause us to come to ourself, when we find that we are in the pig pen of life. You cause us to return unto You.

You receive us with great joy. In Jesus' Name, Amen.

God's Love

"But God commendeth His love toward us, in that, while we were yet sinners, Christ died for us." (Romans 5:8 KJV)

Two stories come to mind when I think about God's love. One happened many years ago, but the message, the revelation, remains a constant in my heart. I recall watching my, then, 18-month-old son playing in our small living room. At that moment, such love rose up in my heart for my child. I said in my heart, *Nothing you could ever do could make me stop loving you,* **ever.** As I continued to watch his exploration, through tears I immediately heard in my heart- *That's how I love you, my child.*

In that one moment, years of wrong mindsets were broken off me as I realized that I would always be God's child; that status does not change through sin or wrong choices. Just as, in the natural, a child who strays or gets off course is still our child. Our love for them is not determined by their behavior. We love our children unconditionally. What joy and rest to know that God's love does not change. His love for us does not depend on our works or good choices. We do **not** have to strive to make God love us. He loves us right where we are. **Take a moment, rest in that knowledge, and know that you are loved, right where you are- right now.**

Sin does put a gap, a distance, between us and God. However, we are still His child, much like the prodigal son, we can choose to live in the pigpen. But, oh what joy when we come to ourself, and run back to our Father's loving embrace. What rest when we realize He has been waiting, longing, searching for us as lost sheep.

That was several years ago, and God has worked many wonderful works in my heart. I have been blessed to walk through trials, the wilderness, and out to the *Good Land* of His perfect sovereign will for my life. He guided me from the pigpen to the palace. Through it all: through tears, failures, falling, getting back up, going forward, surrendering, hoping, and constant help from a Loving Father— through it all, I always remembered, and still do, the moment, that word- **That's how I love you, my child.**

God is our Heavenly Father. He has good plans for us. He loved us in the pig pen. He loves us now- right where we are. God wants us to have and enjoy an abundant life (see John 10:10). He has good plans for us, to bless us; more that we could ask or think (see Ephesians 3:20).

Prayer

Dear God, I have strayed so very far from your great love for me. I have made so many wrong choices. But at this moment, I see that you love me- right where I am. That understanding gives me new hope; hope I haven't had in a long time. Right now, Dear God, I am coming home, I am running to your loving embrace. I know you will receive me with open arms. I surrender my heart, and life to you, right now. I love You, and praise. In Jesus' Name, Amen.

A Mother's Plea

. . . "Looking unto Jesus the author and finisher of our faith, who for the joy that was set before Him endured the cross, despising the shame, and is set down at the right hand of the throne of God."
(Hebrews 12:2 KJV)

Flipping through the channels one evening, a program caught my attention. The episode featured a mother pleading for her young son. They were visiting another country. Apparently, the boy had been accused of stealing and vandalizing a vehicle. I paused my channel surfing to listen. The mother shared her son's verdict and impending sentencing. For his crime, he was facing a caning, a sort of whipping. The punishment involved wrapping his body to protect vital organs.

The mother said her young son was very depressed as the day of the sentencing approached.

I wept with the mother as she continued to share her story. I began to ponder what I would do if it were either of my sons. Immediately I knew. . . I would say, "Take *me, spare my child, I will gladly take his place!*" I felt sure, at that moment, that the young mother would have taken her son's place, were it at all possible.

Dwelling on the scene, immediately I heard that still, small voice in my heart- **That's what I did for you, my child**. More tears, as I pondered, *Jesus took my place, wow! He took your place. It was as if He said: Don't take them; take me. Even though they deserve it, I will take their punishment.* He loved us so much that it was a *joy* to spare us and take our place.

> *Jesus paid it all,*
> *All to Him I owe.*
> *Sin had left a crimson stain,*
> *He washed it white as snow.*

Praise

Thank you, Dear God for Jesus; for loving us so much that You gave Your *only begotten son, (see John 3:16)* to suffer and die in our place.

Who, *through the joy that was set before Him endured the cross. (See Hebrews 12:2) and took our place.*

Happy Thought
You are God's Beloved.
(See Song of Solomon 6:3)

Chapter 2

Lean on God to Laugh, Rest, Hope, Trust, and Walk in Joy Always

"A merry heart does good like a medicine: . . ." (Proverbs 17:22)

Early one morning while emptying my husband's trash can, (his side of the king-sized bed), I tripped. Looking down, I saw the reason-shoes and socks sprawled out in the small space between the bed and his many side tables. Keeping it light, I said to my still resting husband, "Honey, every time I come to your side of the bed, I trip. Do you know why that is?" Without missing a beat, my clever husband responded, "Because you're clumsy?" (A good place to insert LOL)

Laughter is indeed good medicine. We should seek to laugh, daily. As

much as possible, spend time with
people who make you happy,
choose joyful friends, watch a funny
show, buy a laugh box, (those things
are hilarious), watch monkey videos-
you get the picture.

Whenever my family gets together, I
ask God to please send the laughter.
Many times, we find ourselves
laughing so hard we, jokingly, beg to
stop. The Bible says laughter is good
like a medicine. (See Proverbs 17:22)
I believe laughter is healing
medicine to our heart, body, and
soul.

When our hope and trust is in God,
we can indeed laugh, relax, and
walk in joy and peace. We can
enjoy every day, every moment of
our life, when we rest in God's
sovereign will for our lives. God
perfects that which concerns us,
(see Psalms 138:8); gives us beauty
for ashes, (see Isaiah 61:3); makes

straight our paths, (see Proverbs 3:6); and gives us the desires of our heart. (see Psalms 37:4).

Charles Stanley says, "Jesus came to take away our guilt, (see Isaiah 53:10), and the Spirit filled life is designed to overflow with joy and peace." (828)

*"Now may the God of hope fill You with all
Joy and peace in believing,
that you may abound in hope by the
power of the Holy Spirit."
(Romans 15:13 NKJV)
"May the God of hope fill you with all joy
and peace as you trust in Him, so that you
may overflow with hope by the power of
the Holy Spirit."
(Romans 15:13 NIV)*

Joyce Meyer writes in her book, *Seven Things That Steal Your Joy,* that joy is a fruit of the Spirit that dwells in every believer's heart. However, it is released only by making a decision not to allow adverse circumstances to rule our

emotional and mental attitudes. . .
*You have the ability to release and
maintain joy in your life. (Page 192)*
God has equipped us, given us, the
tools we need to do all He bids us
do. By leaning on Him, abiding in
Him, meditating in His Word, we can
release the joy that we already
have. We can choose joy in every
circumstance- *Believing releases joy.*
(192)

Learning to lean on God begins with
prayer and confession-
acknowledging that you can do
nothing apart from God. It begins by
resting in the free gift of grace to live
one day at a time, in hope, joy and
happiness. *Acknowledge God and
He will direct your paths.*
(see Proverbs 3:6)

Prayer

Dear God, I praise You and thank
You. You are my help and hope. You

bless me to choose joy in every circumstance, every day. I look to You and lean on You with Your help. My eyes are on You. You are the one that causes me to overcome all things. Today and every day I choose joy. I choose to trust and obey all You bid me do that I might have life; and that more abundantly (See John 10:10). You are my constant help; my joy is in You. I rest in Your perfect will for my life. You are my hope; my help is in You. In Jesus' Name, Amen.

Lean on God

> ➤ It came to pass after this also, that the children of Moab, the Children of Ammon, and with them *other* beside the Ammonites came against Jehoshaphat to battle.
> ➤ Then there came some that told Jehoshaphat, saying,

There cometh a great multitude against thee from beyond the sea on this side Syria; and, behold, they *be* in Haazazon-tamar, which *is* Engedi.

> And Jehoshaphat feared, and set himself to seek the Lord, and proclaimed a fast throughout all Judah.

> And Judah gathered themselves together, to ask help of the Lord: even out of all the cities of Judah they came to seek the Lord.

> And Jehoshaphat stood in the congregation of Judah and Jerusalem, in the house of the Lord, before the new court,

> And said, O Lord God of our fathers, art thou not God in Heaven?

> And in thine hand is there not power and might, so that none is able to withstand thee?

> Art not thou our God, who didst drive out the inhabitants of this

land before thy people Israel and gavest it to the seed of Abraham thy friend forever?

➤ And they dwelt therein, and have built thee a sanctuary therein for thy name, saying, If, *when* evil cometh upon us, *as* the sword, judgement, or pestilence, or famine, we stand before this house, and in thy presence, (for thy name *is* in this house) and cry unto thee in our affliction, then thou wilt hear and help.

➤ And now, behold, the children of Ammon and Moab and Mount Seir, whom thou wouldest not let Israel invade, when they came out of the land of Egypt, but they turned from them, and destroyed them not;

➤ Our God, wilt thou not judge them? For we have no might against this great company that cometh against us; neither know we what to do; but our

eyes are upon thee.
(2 Chronicles 20:1-10;12 KJV)

"... *We don't know what to do, but our
eyes are on You."*
(2 Chronicles 20:12 NIV)

Sometimes God blesses us to walk through a place where we are totally dependent on Him. We realize that we cannot make it through without His help. Much like Jehoshaphat, and the people of Judah when facing a *great multitude* coming up against them. (See 2 Chronicles 20:2). Like the people of Judah, we see God's provision and faithfulness as we look to Him to do what we cannot do on our own. We see His love and care for us. We truly begin to understand that we are His beloved. We become as little children, totally dependent on our loving Heavenly Father. We learn to lean on Him and look to Him to bring us safely to the other side. We learn to rest in Him to supply all our needs, fulfill our petitions, and walk in joy and peace during uncertain, trying times. Learning to lean on God is vital to keeping our peace, joy and happiness-- always. God takes the ugly that we face and makes it beautiful. We can look to and lean on Him to *perfect that which concerns us* and make *all things work together for our good*. He is our hope in the midst of pain and suffering. He is our help, strength and joy, always.

Note the verse- Jehoshaphat **feared** and set himself to seek the Lord. . . (vs 3) Jehoshaphat did not fear and then make a plan of attack. He did not lean on his own human reason, or strength as a great leader and king. No, we see in the verse that he and all of Judah, sought the Lord, He acknowledged that he didn't know what to do. He humbled himself before God and cried out for help.

We see in verse 15, that God heard and answered their cries; . . .*Thus saith the Lord unto you, be not afraid or dismayed by reason of this great multitude; for the battle is not yours, but God's.* God continues to instruct and comfort them as we note in verse 17; *Ye shall not need to fight in this battle; set yourselves, stand ye still, and see the salvation of the Lord with you.*

It is during times of testing or crisis that we learn to lean on God. When faced with a situation, problem, crisis, or other we can follow the same formula found in 2 Chronicles 20:1-30. We acknowledge the situation; we acknowledge (cry out to) God; we recall all the wonderous works He has done in our lives and throughout scripture; we listen, and hearken to His voice, and with His help, we do all He instructs us to do; we praise God for His help; and finally, we rest.

(So the realm of Jehoshaphat was quiet; for his God gave him rest round about.) 2 Chronicles 20:30

Rise up/ Take A Firm Stand

Walking through a time that I didn't see coming, I found myself going from faith to fear. Sitting on my back porch one evening, with a pumpkin latte and many tears, I began reliving the events of the past week; I recalled moments when I felt afraid; wondering what now; what if? I looked back on the times I cried out unsure of how the situation would evolve. I honestly didn't know what to do. A thought dropped in my heart at that moment: *Rise up- take a firm stand.*

 Pondering that thought, I began to realize that I needed to stop reasoning and recognize that God was in control. He allowed this time for a reason, and a season.

No doubt it was a season of growth; a season to learn to lean on God to see me safely through to the other side. It was an opportunity to rejoice in the midst of the storm, and choose joy, hope and happiness, in spite of my circumstances.

Remembering the first thing Jehoshaphat did- I knew what I needed to do. I had to get my eyes off my circumstances and back on God. I began by pouring out my heart before Him, through tears. I confessed that I didn't know what to do, but my eyes were on Him. I thanked Him for having a plan, a good plan for my life. I acknowledged that He allowed this for a reason and was indeed working a good work in my life through this circumstance. I didn't know how, at that moment, the situation would work out, but I felt the load of worry lift off me. I knew going forward there would be uncertain times- such is the way of growth; however, I knew I would look to God to walk me through each day, one day at a time, and teach me how to lean on Him, rejoice in Him in the midst of trouble, and walk in joy, happiness, and hope. Did that mean there would be no more occasion for tears and pumpkin lattes? No indeed! Like my sister often says to her Heavenly Father during a crisis- "Lord I'm gonna cry now, and that's ok, I think."

Prayer

Dear God, help me lean on You for hope, joy, and happiness during this uncertain time. You are my strength (See Psalms 18:1-2), my high tower (Psalms 144:2), and my defense (Psalms 94:22). I look to You for Your good and wonderful plan during this trying time in my life. I will indeed rejoice in the work of Your hands. Thank You that You are teaching me to lean on You. Thank You for Your grace which is sufficient for me today. Your mercies are new every morning. (See Lamentations 3:22-23).

Please strengthen and help me as I face this situation, worry, or concern. I ask for Your sovereign will in this matter. If it is of no benefit to me, please move it from me. If it is a time that You have ordained, bless me with strength from on high to rejoice in the midst of the storm, and to keep my eyes and heart fixed on You.

I thank You that You are in control. You order my steps. You are my Good Shepherd. You set me on the high places where I shall not be moved. You pick me up when I fall. You are the lifter of my head.

During this time, and always, bless me with the peace that passes understanding. Guard my heart and mind through Christ Jesus. In Jesus' Name, Amen. (See Philippians 4:6&7)

Verses

"Rejoice in the Lord alway: and again I say, Rejoice." (Philippians 4:4; KJV)

"Do not be anxious about anything, but in every situation, by prayer and petition, with thanksgiving, present your request to God. And the peace of God, which transcends all understanding, will guard your hearts and your minds in Christ Jesus." (Philippians 4:6-7; NIV)

Footnote

My son asked about my writing this morning. I shared with him that I had just finished chapter two. I explained that it was a hard chapter to write as I was walking through the events as I wrote them and didn't have the joy of being on the other side of them yet. Immediately, my own writing came back to my heart- You don't have to wait until your worry, care, or concern is behind you; until the time that God has brought you out. By leaning on God, you can choose joy, hope, and happiness even while you have a problem. You can laugh, and rest in your Father's plan during a trying season. Message received.

Happy Thought
That setback is a setup- to propel you to the next level.

Chapter 3

God is Bigger/ Fight or Flight

What if Jehoshaphat and the tribe of Judah had fled when faced with the *vast* army? (See Chapter Two) Are we to run/ flee from the battles we face? Or are we to get before God, cry out to Him; lean on Him; stay at rest; and do all He bids us do; in the face of an unexpected battle?

Jehoshaphat's army did not choose to flee. Instead, they chose to stand still with their eyes firmly fixed on God. They knew they were helpless in their own strength. They understood that God was bigger than any battle; any enemy they faced. They chose to acknowledge Him in their plight and God indeed made a way of escape.

Soldiers are made on the battlefield. That is where we learn to lean on, trust in, hope in, and rejoice in our loving Heavenly Father. That is where we grow and know our Father's protection, grace, and mercy. Surely, He holds us up; strengthens and hardens us to difficulty; and causes us to overcome all things. God equips us to walk through uncertain, difficult times with hope, joy, and happiness. It is in the **battles** we face that we learn to stand strong.

Verses

. . ."Thus saith the Lord unto you, be not afraid or dismayed by reason of this great multitude; for the battle is not yours, but God's."
(2 Chronicles 20:15 KJV)

"Ye shall not need to fight in this battle; set yourselves, stand ye still, and see the salvation of the Lord with you . . ."
(2 Chronicles 20:17)

The Safest Place To Be Is In God's Will

I recall a scene from one of my favorite non-fiction books, *The Hiding Place; Corrie Ten Boom.* The book depicts the events during World War II, and the Nazi Death Camps. Through the horror we see depicted in the book, I often marvel that joy and hope permeates every chapter and event.

In the chapter titled *Invasion,* Holland has just surrendered to the Germans. The night sky was ablaze with war. Corrie was shaken because a shrapnel shard fell in her bed just after she rose, to go to the kitchen. Corrie recalls the event: (Beji; in Holland)

> ➢ The Germans had repaired the bomb damage to the airport (Holland) and were using it now for a base for air raids against England. Night after night we lay in bed listening to the growl

of engines heading west. Occasionally English planes retaliated and then the German fighters might intercept right over Haarlem. (Holland)

> One night I tossed for an hour while dogfights raged overhead, streaking my patch of sky with fire. At last I heard Betsie stirring in the kitchen and ran down to join her.

> She was making tea. She brought it into the dining room where we had covered the windows with heavy black paper and set out the best cups. Somewhere in the night there was an explosion; the dishes in the cupboard rattled. For an hour we sipped our tea and talked, until the sound of planes died away and the sky was silent.

> I said goodnight to Betsie at the door to Tante Jan's rooms and groped my way up the dark

stairs to my own room. The fiery light was gone from the sky. I felt for my bed: there was the pillow. Then in the darkness my hand closed over something hard. Sharp too! I felt blood trickle along a finger. It was a jagged piece of metal ten inches long. "Betsie!"

➤ I raced down the stairs with the shrapnel shard in my hand, We went back to the dining room and stared at it in the light while Betsie bandaged my hand. "On your pillow," she kept saying.

➤ "Betsie, If I hadn't heard you in the kitchen…" But Betsie put a finger to my mouth. "Don't say it Corrie! There are no 'ifs' in God's world. And no places that are safer than other places. **The center of His will is our only safety**- Oh Corrie, let us pray that we may always know it!" (pgs. 83-84)

When we know we are hand placed by God, in the center of His perfect plan and will, we have peace no matter the storm. We know He will provide, protect, and guide us safely to the other side. We need only to lean on Him. We can have joy and peace knowing He is indeed in control, and His plans for us are for good and not evil. (See Jeremiah 29:11 NIV). Indeed, the safest place to be is in the center of God's will.

God is bigger than any battle or situation that we could ever face. We can rest in Him—His sovereign will and purpose. He is our loving Heavenly Father. He is an ever-present help in trouble. He is our strength, our high tower, our joy is in Him, always. Our only position when facing opposition: stand firm, look to God, ask for His help, lean on Him, rejoice, rest, and trust His plan.

Verses

*"But You, O Lord, are a shield for me,
My glory and the One who lifts up my
head." (Psalms 3:3 NKJV)*

*"I will both lie down in peace, and sleep;
For You alone, O Lord, make me dwell in
safety." (Psalms 4:8 NKJV)*

*"But let all those rejoice who put their trust
in You: Let them ever shout for joy,
because You defend them; Let those also
who love Your name be joyful in You.
For You, O Lord, will bless the righteous;
With favor You will surround him as with a
shield."
(Psalms 5:11-12 NKJV)*

Mom's Story

"Keep your eyes on me," I jokingly instructed my mother, sister, and niece Bryanna. It was the opening night of our church's production of *A Cricket County Weddin'* and it appeared we opened to a packed house; well, that is to say that our church basement was very full.

Backstage, more like behind the kitchen door, I peeked out at the audience. It was so good to see my mom enjoying a hearty laugh. I was so proud to have her in the audience, stylish grey wig and all. I couldn't remember a time that she looked more beautiful.

My church, and especially my Sunday School Class, *Women of Grace*, were especially excited to see my mother. Although they had never met her, they had held her up in prayer for well over a year.

Not long after my mom's diagnosis, she came to my home for a weekend visit. Mom and I always enjoyed our visits together. We were always up early, ready for coffee and conversation. Some mornings we would sit on my front porch, watching the sunrise, laughing, crying, swapping stories. I would jokingly tell her to come up and we'd sit on the front porch and *talk about people*. However, this time was different. This time, my heart was heavy.

During mom's stay, I had some errands to run at the local mall. While there, I heard a young lady call her mom. She had found the perfect shoe and wanted to show her mom. The scene pierced my heart as I pondered how much longer I had to share with my mom. I headed home with a troubled heart.

That night, mom and I retired early, weary from a long day. Somewhere in the night I woke up. Recalling the events of the day before, I set about thinking, worrying, and pondering; imaging life without my dear, sweet, fun-loving mom. Amid my sorrowful thoughts, I heard a word in my heart, there was no mistaking the *still small voice:* "Why are you so cast down

about your mother's condition?"
Through tears I replied with a sob,
"Because cancer is big!" Within
moments I heard, "But I am bigger."
Peace and comfort immediately
replaced sorrow and sighing. For the
first time since the diagnosis, I felt
peace, comfort, and hope. *God is
bigger*, I pondered the message of
hope. I knew at that moment,
somehow, mom would be okay.
Whatever she had to walk through,
God would see her to the other side;
whole, restored, and in good health.
I finally slept and awoke the next
morning with a new thought and a
lighter heart.

The night before mom's exploratory
surgery, we spent the night at my
brother and sister in law's home. The
we included all my brothers and
sisters; six total, and a host of
grandkids. We had a wonderful time
complete with a cookout and an
over-the-hill birthday party for my
beautiful, older sister. We knew what

we had to face the next day, but tonight we were together, happy.

Bright and early the next morning we loaded our vans and many vehicles. We were an immeasurable caravan stopping together when one vehicle needed gas, blowing our horns at each other, laughing, sharing- a joyous parade. In our vehicle we shared, as we always did on any road trip, memories of other road trips. One of my favorite memories was a certain trip to Florida. I recall traveling the interstate for many, many miles. Common on such a long trip, we noticed the same vehicles, behind or in front of us all along the journey. One vehicle always ended up in front of us, despite the many stops along the way. Our traveling bunch shared a hearty laugh when, after many miles, the people in the car posted a bumper sticker- **Stop picking your nose while driving.** We knew it was a message for mom.

Finally, our caravan arrived at our destination, King's Daughters Hospital. We were a lively bunch invading the small quiet space, serving as a waiting room and reception area. It got so crowded and chaotic, that the exasperated receptionist finally said, "Okay, anyone who is not with Joann New, please step to the left."

Mom's surgery went very well. We were thankful and relieved when she woke up from the tenacious procedure. Several cancerous tumors were removed. One, however, was wrapped around an artery. Still, we saw the procedure as a success. We knew the next step would be chemo. Through it all, I held the precious thought in my heart- God is bigger.

Piling into our respective vehicles, all our thoughts were on mom, and the night she would need to face. We knew she would be exhausted, and not able to eat or enjoy any festivities as was the night before. Heading home I recall counting the number of cars and vans. At that point others had joined the parade. I counted ten cars to the best of my memory. However, during the ride, one van went missing. Filled with concern, I suddenly realized it was the vehicle containing my mom. We later found out that she had gotten hungry and asked my brother to stop for a fish sandwich!

Mom absolutely came on the other side of that challenge—cancer free and happy in her God. As I look back, I marvel at all she went through: the chemo, surgery, loss of hair. She went through it all with joy, strength, and a wonderful sense of humor. If anyone was downcast around her, she would find a way to cheer them up. I look back in amazement at that trying time. I often ponder how it was possible that we rejoiced and celebrated, as a family, during such a difficult, uncertain time. But even as I wonder, I already know the answer, as once again I recall the words from that night so long ago:

"But I am bigger."

"God is a very present help in trouble."
(See Psalms 46:1)

Happy Thought
Nothing reaches us unless it is
filtered through God's hands first.

Chapter 4

Guard Your Thoughts, And Rest in the Fire

"Be anxious for nothing, but in everything by prayer and supplication, with thanksgiving, let your request be known to God; and the peace of God, which surpasses all understanding, will guard your hearts and minds through Christ Jesus. (Philippians 4:6-7 NKJV)

Finally, brethren, whatever things are true, whatever things are noble, whatever things are just, whatever things are pure, whatever things are lovely, whatever things are of good report, if there is any virtue and if there is anything praiseworthy- meditate on these things." (Philippians 4:8 NKJV)

It is imperative that we learn to think right thoughts, on purpose. The Bible instructs us to take every thought captive. (See II Corinthians 10:5) We need to think about what we are thinking about- be mindful before God. By leaning on God, we can learn to walk in today's grace and not think about tomorrow's cares. (See Matthew 6:34) Most thoughts, cares, or scenarios will never come to pass- but can cause you concern if you allow them to linger. We overcome through prayer, asking for God's help to stop dwelling on wrong thoughts, and by confessing that we are leaning on Him for constant help. I have often heard Joyce Meyer say that God put it on her heart, when she was dwelling on a wrong thought, to *just think about something else*.

God is indeed in control and only allows the measure of what He allows to work a work in us. Even then it is filtered through our loving Heavenly Father's hands. We can rest and trust His good and wonderful plan for us every day of our lives. We can choose, by leaning on God, to think right thoughts on purpose.

We can lean on God to choose joy, rest, hope, happiness, and right thoughts, every day in every situation, even in the midst of the fire.

One word God laid on my heart when I found myself dwelling on a wrong, troubling thought was- *All you need to do is stop thinking about it.*

Several times I have heard in my spirit- *Get that thought off you.* When I hear that, I know I need to get before God and release the wrong thought through *prayer and supplication.* Sometimes if I feel a thought has taken root, I will get before God and cry out to him to uproot it.

My good friend and prayer partner, Virginia Bailey, shared this prayer that God had given her, many years ago. Through the years God has added to the prayer as He blesses me to pray it. (Added part italics)

Prayer

Dear God sever the root, *seedling, sapling,* deep root, hidden root, fresh root, off shoot, crawling root, and *strong root,* of that thought. Pluck it up, turn it upside down, shake it out, leave nothing breathing to take on new life and new root. Renew a right spirit, a clean heart, and a right mind set in me. Shut those doors *(to the wrong thought or thinking)* and seal them tight *forever* with the Blood of Jesus. In Jesus' Name, Amen.

Foolish Fable

I read an old fable many, many years ago. Although it is silly, it does speak volumes of the many worries and cares we choose to allow to trouble our own minds and hearts.

The story goes that a young maiden *(yes maiden; I warned you it was old)* was sobbing uncontrollably and refused to be consoled. Her intended (promised husband), demanded to know the nature of her distress. Try as he might he could not calm the maiden. Through sobs, she explained that someone had thrown an axe up into their main room ceiling. It had gotten stuck and apparently no one bothered to get it down. (Okay- I know, who throws axes in the house, right?) She continued to explain that someday they would have a child. The maiden was sure that the axe would fall on their child's head, killing him instantly. She continued her sobbing and lamenting until the intended husband could stand it no more.

He was so baffled that he told her he was going on a long discovery trip. If he could find three people sillier than her, he would return and marry her. If he could not, he would break off their nuptials. As the story goes, he did indeed find the three and returned home to his beloved. Hopefully they lived happily ever after, maybe.

However ridiculous, the fable does shed light on our own foolish thoughts and imaginations, at times.

Rest

"God is our refuge and strength, A very present help in trouble."
(Psalms 46:1)

"Take My yoke upon you and learn of Me; for I am meek and lowly in heart; and ye shall find rest unto your souls."
(Matthew 11:29)

God is our defense, our always help. (See Psalms 7:10) No matter the situation, He is always with us, strengthening us, giving us grace for each day and hardening us to difficulties.

We can choose to be happy, much like a little child, resting in His help, provision, and tender care. We can cast our cares on Him, for He cares for us. (See 1Peter 5:7).

I recall a day of being so very hurt and confused by a situation at work. Carrying my burden home, I made my way to my treehouse, pumpkin spice latte in hand. Once I reached the top, I poised myself to pour out my complaint through many tears and grumblings. Before I uttered my first syllable, I heard in my heart- *All I want to hear you say is, I choose joy.* Uh- but- they- hurt. Many tears later- Yes, Lord, I choose joy.

It was as if God was saying- I am your Heavenly Father- I care for you- I will take care of you, and all that concerns you- you can rest, be happy, and choose joy while I fix things for you.

God cleans up our messes. He takes care of all that concerns us much like a loving parent. I imagine, in my mind's eye, a child accidentally breaking a glass. The parent, concerned that the child might get injured by the glass, instructing them to go play, as the parent carefully cleans up the mess.

What joy to know that we can come to God, bring Him our mess, and look to Him to fix what we cannot. What joy to just rest and trust and know it is in our loving Father's care. We can indeed go out and play: we can enjoy our life while we have a problem.

Why would we ever choose to sit and worry, fret, and be cast down when our Loving Father takes care of everything that concerns us— always. He instructs us to lean on Him and cast all our burdens upon Him. He is always with us, cares for us, and perfects that which concerns us.

So, rest, rejoice, go out and play. God speaks tenderly to our hearts, as His little children- I will clean up your mess, lean on me, rest in me, choose joy; I will fix this for you, my child.

Flight or Fight/ Rest in the Fire

"When thou passest through the waters, I will be with thee; and through the rivers, they shall not overflow thee: when thou walkest through the fire, thou shalt not be burned; neither shall the flame kindle upon thee." (Isaiah 43:2 KJV)

There was no possible way I could go to the Women's Conference that weekend. The threat of storms had made it nearly impossible; though I was packed and ready to leave as soon as my workday was over. The sky looked ominous the entire day. I had long since given up the notion of the trip. Students were sent home a little early that day, confirming my no travel decision. However, as I was helping to load the buses, a marvelous occurrence happened- the clouds opened up, the sun shone so bright I wish I had brought my sunglasses- No Way! Could it be?

I knew I needed this weekend. I felt I had been walking through the fire and needed some time to cry out to God. I envisioned time alone with God to pour out my complaint. I thought about the many hikes I would take in the beautiful surrounding property, many tears, and mostly an answer to my heart's cry, my longing to step out of my difficult position.

Unsure, I headed out on the two- hour trip to Parchment Valley. I knew it was impossible, in light of the threat of storms, that I had sunshine, bright sunshine. I marveled and took a measure of comfort in the thought that maybe- just maybe- God had made a way for me to go.

Arriving at the conference, I met with a precious group of ladies from Crum Missionary Baptist Church. Although I went alone, I was not alone from the moment I arrived. It was as if God had placed a family for me. They took me under their wings. We rode together, ate together, prayed, laughed, and cried together. I knew we had made lifelong friendships. Even in the fire God gives us surprises, helps, and joys.

The first night, the praise and worship surrounded my heart giving me comfort, hope, and joy in the difficult time. I was amazed that God made a way for me to attend something I needed so desperately. I rejoiced with my new church family during the evening praise and worship.

The next day provided the perfect opportunity for my much-needed hike. Finding a rugged, hand hewed amphitheater, (fire pit surrounded by benches), I found the perfect refuge to pour out my heart. I cried to God for answers. Weary of my current challenging position, longing to move into the next thing I knew He had for me, troubled, and unsure. On and on I prayed with only the birds and an occasional squirrel as an audience.

That night, the keynote speaker ended with- *If you are weary, come forth for prayer.* Not only did I go, but I took two new sisters with me, asking them what they were also weary about.

Even before I reached the altar, I knew the answer— deep in my heart I knew. I realized afresh that I just needed to surrender my heart in the matter. I knew God was bidding me to stay put and do it with joy and happiness. I knew, but needed confirmation, tears, and refreshment Through it all- the tears, the- *but it is too hard*; the- *I cant's*; God was assuring me that He was my strength. He was causing me to lean on Him, and rest in the fire. During that time, I heard a word in my heart- *You can be happy or sad.* I knew I would choose happy.

I knew I still longed to leave my position, that had not changed. But I understood that God was bidding me to choose to be happy right where I was. He would, indeed, move me when it was time. I chose happy. I chose not to *grow weary in well doing*, and to rest in the fire. Finally, my heart rested and I could smile again, and shed happy tears. I knew the situation had not changed, but God had changed me in the midst of the fire.

Later that night, at the campfire singalong, the singer invited testimonies- what we had received that weekend. I didn't hesitate to speak up. I shared my position and how challenging it was. I shared that

I knew God had me there for a season and I concluded through prayer and tears that I would rejoice and do all He bid me do with great joy. I evoked laughter when I shared, "But when it is time to go, I am gonna dance my way out of there." (It was funnier with the motions, sorry.)

Though my position is still hard, I know God hardens me to difficulties. He is my strength and invites me *to take His yoke upon me*. My prayer now- Dear God, when it is time to go, please make it so clear that there is no room for doubt. Swing the door open wide and let me go through with joy, hope, and happiness.

If you are currently walking through the fire, dear reader, oh what a time! God loves you so very much that He has chosen this time to work a wonderful work in your heart; even if it is a fire you started yourself. WOW!

You can indeed rest in His perfect plan. And can I tell you, you will come out on the other side and not even smell like smoke.

You are fearfully and wonderfully made; and God is using this time to bring you unto Himself. (More than ever before) God uses the fire to reveal His love and tender mercies in a wonderful new way. He is teaching you to lean on Him on a higher level. God places us on the high places, where we will not be moved. Our fires and trials cause us to develop hinds' feet, so that we can climb up higher. (See Psalms 18:33 KJV)

I recall many years ago when I was walking through my own fire, I was building a house and suffered many thefts and losses. Because I chose to act as my own contractor, I made many mistakes and had to confront many situations head on. It was indeed a troubling time, a fire.

I felt I had missed God's timing in my eagerness to get started and things did not go smoothly, ever.

My Sunday school teacher at the time, Nancy Ramey, always reminds me of my words on a particular Sunday. As I entered the classroom that morning, Nancy asked how it was going. She knew I was building a house and facing many trials. She was looking for an update. It came as no surprise to her when I responded that I had been through the fire. However, she took great delight in my added response- but I don't even smell like smoke.

God was indeed with me, despite the many missteps I made during the building of my house. He came along and fixed my messes, every time. After the job was done, we had a beautiful two story home complete with, my favorite, a huge, covered porch to enjoy those pumpkin spice latte moments and prayer.

You know the story- The Hebrew children thrown into the fire. But did you know the fire only consumed their shackles, and that they came out of the fire without even the smell of smoke? And in the fire, there was a fourth man. They were not alone for Jesus was with them in the fiery flames. (Daniel 3:24-27)

God's fire, that He allows, serves only to burn the shackles in our heart, and He walks with us through every moment. And indeed, when we come out, we don't even smell like smoke. We come out better than we go in. We can rest, and enjoy life, even in the flames. WOW!

Prayer

Dear God, though the heat of the fire I am walking through has been turned up many times hotter, though I don't understand this time, or how it could possibly work for my good, I know that all You want me to say is- I trust You, Dear God. I rejoice in Your good and wonderful plan for my life, I choose joy. I thank You for all You are doing in my heart and life during this time. I will, indeed, come out better than I went in. In Jesus' Name.

Verses

Although the fig tree shall not blossom,
Neither shall fruit be in the vines;
The labour of the olive fail,
And the fields yield no meat;
The flock shall be cut off from the fold,
And there shall be no herd in the stalls:
Yet I will rejoice in the Lord,
I will find joy in the God of my salvation.
The Lord God is my strength,
And He will make my feet like hinds' feet,
And He will make me walk upon my high places. . . (Habakkuk 3:17-19 KJV)

Come unto Me, all ye that labour and are heavy laden, and I will give you rest. (Matthew 11:28 KJV)

For thou hast made him a little lower than the angels, and hast crowned him with glory and honor. (Psalms 8:5 KJV)

Quote from *Restore My Soul, The Power & Promise of 30 Psalms* by Laura L. Smith

---

Happy Thought
On the darkest days when I feel inadequate, unloved, and unworthy, I remember whose daughter (*son*) I am, and I straighten my crown!

Chapter 5

Release, Surrender, and Receive

"Behold, I stand at the door, and knock; if any man hear my voice, and open the door, I will come in to him, and sup with him, and he with me."
Revelation 3:20 KJV

The Dream

The Rooms of our Heart

One night, I had a dream. I found myself walking through the rooms of what seemed to be a large, beautiful house. I recall walking into one room in particular- a bathroom. In this room, I noticed that every fixture was overlayed with pure gold. It was a room that was more lovely than I had ever seen. As I continued my journey through many more meticulous rooms, I was amazed at the vast riches I saw- the careful attention to detail, the beauty, the gold. I continued wandering in awe taking in the beautiful scene of each room, enjoying the beauty and magnificent details.

Suddenly, however, the scene changed. I found myself in a dark, musky stairwell. The peeling paint; ugly green hues, showing wear of many years gone by. Walking upward I was greeted by a single, dingy door to the right. As the door opened, I noticed that it was a sort of eating establishment. Before I could take in all my surroundings, however, an angry cook, holding a black cast iron skillet, pointed his boney finger at me and screamed, "Get out of here!"

I awoke and marveled at the details of the vivid dream. Realizing the dream must surely have a meaning, I began to pray for understanding. I asked God for the revelation. I began to understand that each room represented a room in my own heart. The rooms that were beautiful, overlayed with pure gold, were rooms I had opened to God. He had come in and made each room beautiful, and whole, a joy to enter.

But what about the ugly stairwell and the angry cook, I continued to pray. Immediately the understanding dropped into my heart- That room, I heard, was the rejection room. All the rejections I had faced in my life-every time I was made to feel *not good enough*; not part of a group; rejected by a prospective employer; jilted by a boyfriend; overlooked and cast aside- I had locked up tight in that room. I had locked the door tight and never opened it to God.

At that moment, the understanding surrounded my heart- If we keep doors shut to God, we suffer the consequences. When we refuse to open these hurtful, angry, bitter doors, we experience many side effects- depression, anger, bitterness, anxiety, lack of self-esteem, fear of rejection, and a host of other emotions. But glory to God as we open these doors wide and let the light of His love in, we begin to be renewed. God cleanses those rooms and makes everything beautiful-restoring them to their original glory and intent. Our job: open the doors, release the key to God, and invite Him in through prayer and supplication.

Prayer

Thank you, Dear God, for revealing the contents of my heart. At this moment I am ready to, with your help, open the doors wide. I know You will make the ugly rooms beautiful again, overlaid with gold and jewels. I surrender the keys to the rooms that I have shut off for so long. I want to be happy in You. I choose to open the doors wide and let the light of your love shine in. No more dark rooms in my heart; I will walk in the light of Your love every day of my life, from this point on. I love You and praise You. I choose joy, hope and happiness. In Jesus' Name, Amen.

It's Time To Face It

It was the first night of our church conference. Arriving early, I reached out to open the front door. However, before I could even step inside a thought surrounded my heart – *It's time to face it.* Oh no! I knew what the **it** was. I had shut the door to a hurt (buried it) so very long ago. I knew God had chosen that moment to bring it to the surface.

Walking into the church and taking a seat in the back, I heard God speak to my heart concerning the matter. I understood as never before that I had strayed from His perfect plan, in an area, and suffered loss and missed out on many joyful blessings.

God had chosen that time, that moment. Immediately, I saw in my spirit, a huge black cloud rising out of me- I cried out, in my heart- *Oh no Dear God- it's too hard.* I had never experienced anything like it before, but I knew God was causing me to face and overcome a hurt buried so very long ago. It was easier, I thought, to let it lie dormant than to face the hurt and acknowledge the huge loss and hopelessness of the dead dream. But those were my thoughts. God's thoughts are higher than ours. (See Isaiah 55:9)

I knew somehow that I could no longer keep the door shut on the hurt. I realized in my heart that it was time, and somehow, I could indeed face it.

Okay Lord, I am ready. It was, no doubt, going to be painful, maybe more than I could bear. However, I was confident that because it was time, God would help me recover.

Yes, Lord, I strayed from Your Good plan, I began to acknowledge, I lost the dream You placed in my heart. I have no hope of recovery. As I faced the hurt and began to acknowledge my sin before God and accepted His forgiveness, something amazing happened—I smiled. The burden was lifted; the door flung open. The huge load of guilt was gone. My heart was lighter, and I smiled. The very thing I kept hidden had kept my heart captive. But by releasing the burden of sin I was set free to hope, yet again, in God's mercy, grace, forgiveness, and restoration. I smiled through sweet tears.

I didn't know how, or even if I was completely right, but somehow, I had a glimmer of hope that God would restore the huge loss, dream, and longing. Somehow, even though I was the one who threw down the dream, the promise, I dared to hope, at that moment, that

God would give me what I didn't deserve. Was it possible? For the first time in many, many years I dared to hope in His mercy. For now, however, I smiled- the burden gone, and a glimmer of hope in its place.

Release

I love the story of the little monkeys, selfishly guarding their water source. Villagers seeking water will set up a trap to catch one of the knowledgeable little fellows. They use the monkey's curiosity to trap and trick it into leading them to water. The villager places an object in a small hole in a tree. The curious little monkey will stick its hand in the hole to retrieve it. Because they refuse to let the treasured item go, they become trapped. They struggle and struggle for freedom, all the while holding onto what is keeping them in bondage. By releasing the treasured item, they can easily pull

their hand back out. As a result, they are captured by the villager.
While captive, the monkey is fed a salty diet for a short season. Upon its release, thirsty and tired, it immediately runs to the water source with the villagers in hot pursuit. By this means, the villagers can find an oasis of a new water supply.

Much like the little monkey, we sometimes struggle to break free of whatever is holding us captive. We struggle and struggle to break free and often do not realize that freedom comes when we release and open the door wide to God. We can look to Him as our source, our treasure, our hope. When we cry out to Him through prayer and supplication, we can let go and let God work a wonderful work, a transformation, in our life.

How can we be happy God's way- by releasing what we have been gripping so tightly and walk in the freedom God so freely gives. By opening every door of our heart to a Loving Heavenly Father and inviting Him to come in and make every room in our heart beautiful.

Prayer

I can't, I have struggled for so long. I am like that little monkey refusing to let go. But right now, I invite You, Dear God, into this mess- this messy room. I ask You to make it beautiful. Whatever I have clung to, refused to release, tried to fix on my own, I release to You. Come in and help me let go; help me to hope yet again. Help me release all I have held onto for so long. Help me, Dear God, fling all the doors open in my heart and let the light of Your love come in. Make me brand new in You. In Jesus' Name, Amen.

Verses

"Lay not up for yourselves treasures upon earth, where moth and rust doth corrupt, and where thieves break through and steal: but lay up for yourselves treasures in heaven, where neither moth nor rust doth corrupt, and where thieves do not break through nor steal: for where your treasure is, there will your heart be also."
(Matthew 6:19-21 KJV)

"Ask, and it shall be given you; seek, and ye shall find; knock, and it shall be opened to you: for every one that asketh receiveth; and he that seeketh findeth; and to him that knocketh it shall be opened."
(Matthew 7: 7-8 KJV)

Happy Thought
For where your treasure is,
there will your heart be also.
Matthew 6:21

Chapter 6

Remain Faithful and Joyful, Praise God, and Hope in Affliction

*". . . I made treasurers over the treasuries'
Shelemiah the priest, Zadok the scribe, and
Pedaiah of the Levites; assisting them was
Hanan son of Zaccur, the son of
Mattaniah, for they were counted
faithful . . ."
(Nehemiah 13:13 KJV)*

If you find yourself weary where you are right now: your job, your situation, your location, or other circumstance-the absolute best thing you can do is continue to show up with a good attitude and remain faithful. Choose to remain joyful as you look for and pray for change. Don't just endure but choose to delight in God during the trying situation. Lean on Him to choose joy-right where you are- until God moves you or changes your situation, or changes you in the midst of your circumstances.

According to Joyce Meyer, *sometimes* God tests our faithfulness. He assigns us to do something for a period of time that we do not want to do. Faithfulness is not showing up day after day- faithfulness is showing up with a good attitude and excellent spirit, *each day.*

God sees, knows, and understands your longing. He is ever with you to help, strengthen, and encourage you forward. His grace is sufficient right where you are. You can choose happiness and joy, even when you do not like your surroundings or circumstances.

Garment of Praise

"The Spirit of the Lord God is upon me: because the Lord has anointed me to preach good tidings unto the meek; he hath sent me to bind up the brokenhearted, to proclaim liberty to the captives, and the opening of the prison to them that are bound; to proclaim the

acceptable year of the Lord, and the day of vengeance of our God; to comfort all that mourn; to appoint unto them that mourn in Zion, to give them beauty for ashes, the oil of joy for mourning, the garment of praise for the spirit of heaviness; that they might be called trees of righteousness, the planting of the Lord, that He might be glorified." (Isaiah 61:1-3 KJV)

Asking God to move a situation from me, complaining daily, crying out for change- in the midst I awoke one night around 3:00 am. I immediately began my prayer of complaint. Dear God, this situation is too hard; it is more than I can bear; it is uncomfortable; please make a way for change. I cry out to you, Dear God. On and on I poured out my complaint through many tears. After a few more tearful moments, I heard in my heart - *I am using this situation to work a work in you; then I will move the situation.* I said– *No, move this situation; then work a work in me.* Again, I heard- *I am using this situation; then I will move it.* Again, I responded- *No, please move the difficult situation from me first; then work a work in me.* A third time I heard- *I am using this time to work a work in your heart; then I will move it.* At that point I exclaimed- *Well, I'm just gonna turn over and go back to sleep then!*

But God had a wonderful plan indeed. Going forward, I found myself hitting my knees daily, complaining and asking for change. I thought I just couldn't bear it another day. I recall one day in particular feeling heavyhearted, getting on my knees to pour out my complaint. Before I could utter the first sentence I heard in my heart-Praise Me.

Pause. . . sigh. . . what!?. . . but it was unmistakable- God **was** bidding me to praise Him in the midst of the circumstances. After a short battle, I opened my mouth and was amazed at the praise that poured forth. Needless to say, my heart, my countenance was lifted up. Nothing had changed, but my heart felt lighter somehow. After that, each time I got on my knees I heard- Praise Me. Eventually it became natural to praise instead of complain. Gradually, my situation changed as God moved the burden. I was indeed relieved, but more than that- I was lighter in my spirit. God had given me a *garment of praise for the spirit of heaviness.* I understood why He allowed that terrible time. I came out on the other side grateful for the change He had worked in my heart and life, and even for the difficulty.

Verses

"That He would grant you, according to the riches of His glory, to be strengthened with might by His Spirit in the inner man; that Christ may dwell in your hearts by faith. . ." (Ephesians 3:16-17 KJV)

*"Be joyful in hope, patient in affliction,
faithful in prayer."
(Romans 12:12 NIV)*

Hope in Affliction

In the midst of suffering, during the long roll calls, in the terrible prison camps, (*The Hiding Place*) with just a thin gown between themselves and the bitter temperatures, Corrie and her sister Betsie remained faithful, joyful, and hopeful. They continued to look to God for His help, comfort, and provision. Amid the pain and suffering, Corrie and her sister continued to lean on God. Settling down in their bunks at night they would read scriptures and sing with other bunkmates. You could see the joy and hope they held in their hearts, even when their circumstances were dire. They chose to look to, lean on, and rejoice in their Loving Heavenly Father.

➤ *But as the rest of the world grew strange, one thing became increasingly clear. And that was the reason the two of us were here.*

➤ *Why others should suffer we were not shown. As for us, from morning until lights out, whenever we were not in ranks for roll call, our Bible was the center of an ever-widening circle of help and hope.*

➤ *Like waifs clustered around a blazing fire, we gathered about it, holding out our hearts to its warmth and light.*

➤ *The blacker the night around us grew, the brighter and truer and more beautiful burned the word of God.*

➤ *"Who shall separate us from the love of Christ? Shall tribulation, or distress, or persecution, or famine, or nakedness, or peril, or sword?... Nay, in all these things we are more than*

conquerors through him that
loved us."
➤ I would look about as Betsie
read, watching the light leap
from face to face. More than
conquerors. . . It was not a
wish. It was a fact.
➤ We knew it, we experienced it,
minute by minute- poor, hated,
hungry.
➤ We are more than conquerors.
Not "we shall be." We are!
(The Hiding Place; Pg 206)

Barracks 28

The sisters were indeed hopeful in
affliction. They dreamed of a time
when they could turn their suffering
into a ministry for those affected by
the brutal war and hatred.

➤ "Betsie," I whispered . . ."what
can we do for these people?
Afterward I mean. Can't we

> *make a home for them and*
> *care for them and love them?"*
> ➢ *"Corrie, I pray every day that*
>   *we will be allowed to do this! To*
>   *show them that love is greater!"*
> ➢ *And it wasn't until I was*
>   *gathering twigs later in the*
>   *morning that I realized that I*
>   *had been thinking of the*
>   *feeble-minded, and Betsie*
>   *of their persecutors.*
>   *(Pg 220;221)*

Through it all, Corrie and Betsie remained joyful in affliction by rejoicing in the midst of suffering-thanking God for all things, even the fleas as they kept the guard away from their barracks, allowing them to freely hold their Bible studies.

> ➢ "Fleas!" I cried. "Betsie, the place is swarming with them!"
> ➢ "Betsie how can we live in such a place?"

➢ "Show us, Show us how." It was said so matter of factly, it took me a second to realize she was praying.

➢ "Corrie!" . . . "He has given us the answer! Before we asked, as He always does! In the Bible this morning. Where was it? . ."

➢ I glanced down at the long dim aisle to make sure no guard was in sight, then drew the Bible from its pouch. "It was in First Thessalonians," I said. . . In the feeble light I turned the pages.

➢ Here it is: "Comfort the frightened, help the weak, be patient with everyone. See that none of you repays evil for evil, but always seek to do good to all." It seemed written expressly for Ravensbrück.

> "Go on," said Betsie. "That wasn't all."
> "Oh yes'. . . to one another and to all. Rejoice always, pray constantly, give thanks in all circumstances; for this is the will of God in Christ Jesus."
> "That's it, Corrie! That's His answer. "Give thanks in all circumstances!" That's what we can do. We can start right now to thank God for every single thing about this new barracks!" (Pg 209)
> I stared at her, then around me at the dark, foul-aired room. "Such as?" I asked.
> "Such as being assigned here together."
> I bit my lip. "Oh yes, Lord Jesus!"
> "Such as what you're holding in your hands."

> I looked down at the Bible. "Yes! Thank You, dear Lord that there was no inspection when we entered here! Thank You for all the women here in this room who will meet You in these pages."

> "Yes," said Betsie." Thank You for the very crowding here. Since we're packed so close, that many more will hear!" She looked at me expectantly. "Corrie!" she prodded.

> "Oh, all right. Thank You for the jammed, crammed, stuffed, packed, suffocating crowds."

> "Thank You," Betsie went on serenely," for the fleas and for..."

> The fleas! This was too much. "Betsie, there is no way even God can make me grateful for a flea."

> ➢ "Give thanks in all circumstances," she quoted. "It doesn't say, 'in pleasant circumstances.' Fleas are a part of this place where God has put us."
> ➢ And so we stood between piers of bunks and gave thanks for fleas.
> ➢ But this time I was sure Betsie was wrong. (Pg 210)

Remain Faithful/ Rejoice in all Things

If you don't understand what God is working in your life, or why He has placed you where you are, you can still choose to remain and rejoice, rest and hope. You can choose to rejoice *always, pray constantly, and give thanks in all circumstances. (See First Thessalonians)* You can choose to remember that God has a good plan for all He allows. You can even thank God for the **fleas** in your life, knowing He is in control and has a wonderful plan for you. Remember that He allows the measure of what He allows to work a work in your life, and that under the watchful eye of a loving Heavenly Father.

Chapter 7

Part Two-Remain Faithful, Hopeful and Joyful

Ask God what He is working in your life at this time. Thank Him constantly that He is with you always, and His burden is light.

Rejoice in His watchful care and keeping. Ask Him to help you remain hopeful and joyful during this time, knowing that He has a good plan, is an ever-present help, and will bring you safely to the other side. Remember what God has placed in your heart, He will do.

The Storm

And the same day, when evening was come, he saith unto them,
"Let us pass over to the other side."

- ➢ And there arose a great storm of wind, and the waves beat into the ship, so that it was now full.
- ➢ And he was in the hinder part of the ship, asleep on a pillow: and they awake him, and say unto him, Master, carest thou not that we perish?
- ➢ And he arose, and rebuked the wind, and said to the sea, **Peace, Be still.**
- ➢ And the wind ceased, and there was a great calm.
- ➢ And he said unto them, *Why are ye so fearful? How is it that ye have no faith? (Mark 4: 35,37-40 KJV)*

Jesus said to His disciples- *Let us cross over.* But when the storm arose, they immediately forgot His words. They took their eyes off Him and became fearful. They needed only to recall what Jesus said- *Let us pass over to the other side.*

Jesus rebuked the winds, but He also rebuked his disciples- *Why are you so fearful? How is it that you have no faith?*

When God gives us a word, a promise, we can be sure that He will do what He says He will do. When storms arise, we need only to hold onto the anchor, and cross over. He will take us to the other side and bring us out to a wealthy place. We needn't fear or be dismayed. We can keep our eyes and heart on God and His promises, no matter the storm- **Let us cross over.**

Happy Thought
God will bring us out to a wealthy place, on the other side of the storm.

Verses

*"For thou, O God, hast proved us:
Thou hast tried us, as silver is tried.
Thou broughtest us into the net;
Thou laidst affliction upon our loins.
Thou hast caused men to ride over our
heads; We went through the fire and
through water; but thou broughtest us out
into a wealthy place."*
(Psalms 66: 10-12 KJV)

Prayer

Help me, Dear God, to remain
faithful, hopeful, and joyful always.
Help me to choose joy, even when I
don't understand the time I am
walking through. Help me to always
remember that your burden is light,
and You have good plans for me.
You are bringing me to a *good land*.

You are working a wonderful work in
my life. I rejoice in Your Holy Name.
You are my ever-present help in
trouble. I lean on You and hope in
You, always. *You are my strength,*

my high tower and the lifter of my head. (See Psalms 18:2) I praise You in the midst of the storm. I hope in You. I know You have good plans for me. In Jesus' Name, Amen.

God's Burden is Light/ His Grace is Sufficient

"Come unto me, all ye that labour and are heavy laden, and I will give you rest. Take my yoke upon you and learn of me; for I am meek and lowly in heart; and ye shall find rest unto your souls. For my yoke is easy, and my burden light."
(Matthew 11:28-30 KJV)

If you are carrying a heavy burden, trying to do all you think God bids you do, trying to be joyful, trying to be happy where you are, trying to apply all you know and read—**remember**, God's burden is light. All that God bids you to do He equips, anoints, and gives you the grace to do.

"Abide in me, and I in you. As the branch cannot bear fruit itself, except it abide in the vine. I am the vine, ye are the branches: He that abideth in me, and I in him, the same bringeth forth much fruit: for without me ye can do nothing."
(John 15:4-5 KJV)

He is the vine; we are the branches. Apart from Him, we can do nothing. (See John 15:5) Ask God to teach you how to abide in Him, to choose joy in every situation, how to delight in Him. His grace is sufficient for you. Say to God, Apart from You I can do nothing; by abiding in You, I can do all You bid me do. Teach me to lean on You for all things. I look to You and hope in You. I come unto You with hope and expectation. You are teaching me and causing me to overcome all things. I will rest in You as Your burden is light. You are teaching me to remain frustration free. Leaning on You I will walk in joy, hope, and expectation every day, in every situation, for Your burden is indeed light. I surrender my heart and will to You, with Your help. I take Your yoke upon me just now. In Jesus' Name, Amen."

The Yoke

A yoke is often used to hold two animals together; they share the load- such as plowing the field. Most commonly, especially in Bible times, this involved oxen. Jesus invites us to - **take *My yoke upon you and learn of Me... For My yoke is easy, and My burden light.*** When we are yoked to Jesus our burden is lifted. No longer are we trying to do everything with our own strength, but we are leaning on Him every step of the way.

Prayer if you are heavy laden

Dear God, help me to do all You instruct me to do. I lean on You. I can do nothing apart from You.

I take Your yoke upon me and choose to learn of You. Indeed, Your burden is easy; light. You teach me and instruct my heart in the night seasons. (See Psalms 16:7) You are my constant help. Because You are my constant help, it is not hard to do all You bid me do. I needn't struggle or strain— just lean, trusting You to guide me in the way You would have me go, choosing joy and happiness always. I will rest, play, and enjoy every day because You are in control. You perfect that which concerns me. (See Psalms 138:8) You give me a heart of flesh and cause me to walk in Your ways. I can choose joy, hope, and happiness for You order my steps. In Jesus' Name, Amen.

"A new heart will I give you, and a new spirit will I put within you: and I will take away the stoney heart out of your flesh, and I will give you a heart of flesh. And I will put my spirit within you, and cause you to walk in my statues. . ."
(Ezekiel 36:26-27 KJV)

God's Grace is Sufficient for you

Pray these verses during a trial. Lift your head and rejoice. God's grace is sufficient for you. His burden is light.

Prayer During A Trial

Thou art good, and doest good:
Teach me thy statues.
The proud have forged a lie against me;
but I will keep thy precepts with my whole heart.
Their heart is as fat as grease; but I delight in thy law.
It is good for me that I have been afflicted;
that I might learn thy statues.
The law of thy mouth is better unto me than thousands of gold and silver.
Thy hands have made me and fashioned me; Give me understanding, that I may learn thy commandments.
They that fear thee will be glad when they see me because I have hoped in thy word.
I know, O Lord, that thy judgements are right, and that thou in faithfulness hast afflicted me.

Let, I pray thee, thy merciful kindness be for
my comfort, according to thy word unto
thy servant.
Let thy tender mercies come unto me, that
I may live: for thy law is my delight.
Let the proud be ashamed; for they dealt
perversely without a cause:
but I will meditate in thy precepts.
(Psalms119: 68-78 KJV)

Our only response to a trial, that can
cause our heart to fear, is- I will not
fear. God has placed me; He keeps
me; He rejoices over me with
singing;(See Zephaniah 3:17) He is
my defense and comforts me on
every side; (See Psalms 94:22) He will
work this out for my good; (See
Romans 8:28) I will stand firm in the
power of His might. He will hide me in
the shadow of His wings until these
calamities are overpast. (See Psalms
57:1)

I will lean on the Lord, rejoice, hope,
and choose joy in the midst of the
angry waves and storm. Who am I to

fear what man can do to me and
forget the Lord my maker?
(See Psalms 118:6; Isaiah 51:13)

Remain Faithful in the Midst of the Angry Waves

*"Trust in Him at all times :ye people, pour
out your hearts before Him. God is a refuge
for us. Selah"*
(Psalms 62:8 KJV)

Chapter 8

Conclusion

Throughout this book we have explored many things: God's great love for us all; that He equips us for all things; how to lean on Him for all things; and to choose joy in every situation, with God's help. We have, also, addressed how to guard our thoughts and to rest in the midst of the fire; to release our burdens and receive all God has for us. Finally, we have focused on how to remain faithful during trying situations; to remain faithful, even when things press against us, or we are faced with a storm we did not see coming. (Sometimes God must take us through the storm to get us to the other side.) We have indeed discovered that God **will always** bring us safely to the other side of all situations, and out to a wealthy place; additionally, we see, know, and understand that God's burden is light; all He bids us to do; He helps us to do. He is our constant help.

As this book comes to an end, let's explore one final thought together: **Being Our most beautiful/ most healthy at every age.**
(Please consult your doctor before pursuing any life change such as walking, diet, or other)

One More Story

Many years ago, a desire dropped in my heart- **to be my most beautiful and most healthy at every age.** A rather bold thought at best; yet that bold thought became my prayer. At that moment, I truly desired to do all I could to be healthy all the days of my life, and hey, why not add most beautiful as well. Immediately after my prayer, three life changing things dropped in my heart- eat healthy, walk, and Praise God. I knew God had given me the answer. I knew at that moment I would work toward those goals every day.

When I began my journey, I was a huge carb eater, mostly sweets. I walked moderately, and although I thanked God for answered prayers, I knew I had a lot to learn about praise (See chapter 6- section titled **Garment of Praise)**. Thus began my journey. I began by getting knowledge; reading all that came across my path concerning healthy eating, the benefits of walking, the harmful effects of smoking; (at that time I would smoke, feel concerned about the harmful effects, and lay them back down; a vicious cycle at best).

One author that I found most helpful in my quest towards healthy habits was/is Dr. Colbert. I have often turned to his books and found them to be filled with vital information and motivation. Working toward these goals has been and continues to be a process. I am continually growing in grace and knowledge toward this awesome task.

Very recently, God has impressed on my heart to- *Be consistent.* I know that applies to all God bids me do: choosing joy, walking in hope, doing all I can do to be my most healthy and beautiful at every age, leaning on him, enjoying every day no matter my circumstances, and remembering God is my help and His burden is light. Consistency is the key to walking in constant joy and fellowship with God every day.

Get Knowledge

"The heart of the prudent getteth knowledge; And the ear of the wise seeketh knowledge."
(Proverbs 18:15 KJV)

What now? We continue in the knowledge and wisdom God has imparted to us. We lean on Him;

stand firm, and remain consistent, in all God commands and enables us to do. We remember His words to us; and rejoice in His constant help and provision. We delight in Him; rest in Him; and choose joy every single day with His help- one day a time.

We cast off every burden, remembering that His burden is light. We go out and play, knowing that He cleans up our messes; and that He has a big eraser when we really blow it. We lighten up and become as little children totally enjoying life knowing that our Heavenly Father really does care for us and is always ready to help us. We smile, hope, and rejoice.

We always remember that God is in control of all we walk through. He allows the measure of what He allows to work a work in us. He is in control of the angry waves. He is teaching us to look to Him and lean on Him in the storms of life. He is growing us up and causing us to remain steadfast, hopeful, joyful, patient, and calm.

We remember when, walking through a season of growth, to say- I trust You; I hope in You; I lean on You; You are my constant help; I choose joy right now, even before I have my answer, or deliverance. In this way, God is causing us, teaching us, to always be stable in Him. Indeed, that is true security and joy.

Remember, God's burden is light. It is not a burden to do all He bids us do. He is our constant help, always.

Always Remember
We are not learning to cope but to lean.

1. How very much God loves you- **But God commendeth His love toward us, in that, while we were yet sinners, Christ died for us. (Romans 5:8)**

2. When our hope and trust is in God we can laugh, relax, and rest. We can enjoy every day, every moment of our life, when we rest in His sovereign will for our lives. God perfects that which concerns us (See Psalms 138:8); gives us beauty for ashes (See Isaiah 61:3); makes straight our paths (See Proverbs 3:6); and gives us the desires of our heart (See Psalms 37:4)

3. The safest place to be is in God's will. **But You, O Lord, are a shield for me; my glory and the One who lifts up my head. (Psalms 3:3 NKJV)**

4. Instead of dwelling on a troubling thought- *stop thinking about it*. Ask God to help you. Lean on Him to let the thought go; release it to the *reconciling power of the cross*. **Finally, brethren, whatever things are true, whatever things are noble, whatever things are just,**

whatever things are pure, whatever things are lovely, whatever things are of good report, if there is any virtue and anything praiseworthy, meditate on these things. (Philippians 4:6-8 NKJV)

5. How can we be happy God's way? By releasing what we have been gripping so tight; and opening every room of our heart to God. **Behold, I stand at the door and knock: if any man hear *My voice, and open the door, I will come into him, and sup with him, and he with me. (Revelation 3:20 KJV)***

6. Remain faithful, joyful, and hopeful, even when you do not like your circumstances, and hope strongly for change. **Be joyful in hope, patient in affliction, faithful in prayer. (Romans 12:12 NIV)**

7. If you are carrying a heavy burden, trying to do all you know God bids you to do,

trying to be joyful, trying to be happy where you are, trying to apply all you know and read, **remember—God's Burden is Light.** All that He bids you to do, He equips, anoints, and gives you the grace to do. **Come unto Me, all ye that labour and are heavy laden, and I will give you rest. Take my yoke upon you, and learn of me; for I am meek and lowly in heart; and ye shall rest unto your souls. For my yoke is easy, and my burden light. (Matthew 11:28-30 KJV)**

8. Lean on God to be your most beautiful, most healthy at every age- to walk, enjoy healthy foods, and praise Him, every day.
The Spirit of the Lord God is upon me: because the Lord has anointed me to preach good tidings unto the meek; he hath sent me to bind up the brokenhearted, to proclaim

liberty to the captives, and the opening of the prison to them that are bound; to proclaim the acceptable year of the Lord, and the day of vengeance of our God; to comfort all that mourn; to appoint unto them that mourn in Zion, to give them beauty for ashes, the oil of joy for mourning, the garment of praise for the spirit of heaviness; that they might be called trees of righteousness, the planting of the Lord, that He might be glorified. (Isaiah 61:1-3 KJV) (Ps.139:14 KJV) Beloved, I wish above all things that thou mayest prosper and be in health, even as thy soul prospereth. (3 John 1:2)

9. God is teaching us to overcome all things. He sometimes allows us to walk through situations (storms) to learn to overcome;

to learn to lean on Him, and respond with joy, hope, and expectation.
(1John 5:4); (1 John 4:4) (Revelation 12:11)

10. Stay in balance each day. Keep each day simple by looking to God for His will for your day. Don't over plan, or overburden your day, trying to do too much. Avoid pressure and stress- God help us walk in pleasure not pressure— **One Day at a Time.**

A Prayer when you find yourself overburdened

My precious prayer partner of over thirty years shared this prayer with me.
I have prayed it many times through the years. I continue to pray it when I allow too much in my day and heart – (Prayer shared by Virginia Bailey)

Dear God, sever the root, seedling, sapling, deep root, hidden root, fresh root, off shoot, crawling root, and strong root of the thought (pressure, burden or care) I allowed in my heart and mind.
Pluck them up; turn them upside-down; shake them out; leave nothing breathing to take on new life and new root.
Renew me in the spirit of my mind, create in me a right spirit and a clean heart; and a right mind set. Shut the doors I allowed to open; and seal them tight with the blood of Jesus. In Jesus' Name, Amen.
(See Psalms 51:10)

Some Final Thoughts

Don't reason in your heart- I need to be consistent; I need to choose joy; I need to remember not to grow weary; and on and on. . . Not that these things aren't good to do; indeed, they are- but instead we should say- I lean on You, Dear God, to help me choose joy in this situation; I lean on You not to grow weary in well doing; I lean on You to be consistent in all You bid me do. Also, ask God to show you if you have allowed any thought, circumstance, or emotion to hinder your joy. Ask Him to reveal it that you might, with His help, overcome quickly, and rejoice, yet again, in Him.

Remember God's burden is light. He is our constant help. Look to Him every day for the help and strength you need to walk in joy, hope, and happiness in every situation.

Keep every day simple. Don't try to do too much in one day. Don't try to solve tomorrow's problems today. If it is not a **today** task or thought- don't think or worry about it today. Live joyfully, one day at a time, resting in God's sovereign will for the day you are in.

Verses

*"God is our refuge and strength, a very
present help in trouble."
(Psalms 46:1 KJV)*

*"The Lord is my rock, and my fortress, and
my deliverer, my God, my strength, in
whom I will trust; my buckler, and the horn
of my salvation, and my high tower."
(Psalms 18:2 KJV)*

*"Bless the Lord, O my soul; and all that is
within me, bless his holy name.
Bless the Lord, O my soul, and forget not all
his benefits: Who forgiveth all thine
iniquities; Who healeth all thy diseases;
Who crowneth thee with lovingkindness
and tender mercies; Who satisfies thy
mouth with good things; So that thy youth
is renewed like the eagle's."
(Psalms 103: 1-5 KJV)*

*"In God I will praise His word, In God I have
put my trust; I will not fear what flesh can
do unto me." (Psalms 56:4 KJV)*

*"I will praise Thee; for I am fearfully and
wonderfully made. . ."
(Psalms 139:14 KJV)*

"For thou, O God, hast proved us: Thou hast tried us, as silver is tried.
Thou broughtest us into the net; thou laidst affliction upon our loins.
Thou hast caused men to ride over our heads; We went through fire and through water: But thou broughtest us out into a wealthy place."
(Psalms 66: 10-12 KJV)

"But thou, O Lord, art a shield for me; My glory, and the lifter up of mine head."
(Psalms 3:3 KJV)

"Fear thou not; for I am with thee: be not dismayed; for I am thy God: I will strengthen thee; yea, I will help thee; yea, I will uphold thee with the right hand of my righteousness." (Isaiah 41:10 KJV)

Pray The Word

"Behold, I stand at the door and knock: if any man hear my voice, and open the door, I will come in to him, and sup with him, and he with me."
(Revelation 3:20 KJV)

Dear God, I open every room of my heart to You. Come in and make every room of my heart beautiful before You; that I might praise You, rejoice in You, and hope in You every day. In Jesus' Name, Amen.

"Be anxious for nothing, but in everything by prayer and supplication, with thanksgiving, let your request be known to God; and the peace of God, which surpasses all understanding, will guard your hearts and minds through Christ Jesus." *(Philippians 4:6-7 NKJV)*

Dear God, please strengthen and help me as I face this situation, worry, or concern. I ask for your sovereign will in this situation/ circumstance. If it is no benefit to me, please move it from me. If it is a time that You have ordained, bless me with strength from on high to rejoice in the midst of the storm, and to keep my eyes and heart fixed on You.

I thank You that You are in control; You order my steps; You are my *Good Shepherd.* You set me on the high places where I shall not be moved. You pick me up when I fall. You are the lifter of my head.

During this time, and always, bless me with the peace that passes all understanding. Guard my heart and mind through Christ Jesus. In Jesus' Name, Amen.

"Beloved, I pray that you may prosper in all things and be in health, just as your soul prospers." (III John 1:2)

Dear God, it is Your will that I prosper and walk in good health, as my soul prospers. Please help me, one day at a time, to *walk, eat healthy,* and *praise You.* Bless me to be my most healthy, most beautiful, at every age. In Jesus' Name, Amen.

"Help me, O Lord my God! Oh, save me according to Your mercy."
(Psalms 109:26 NKJV)

A most heartfelt prayer, when you don't know what else to pray- Help me, Dear God. In Jesus' Name, Amen.

Our pastor, Jarrod Belcher (Williamson First Baptist Church), said in a recent message - *One of the greatest things we can aspire to is to be changed by God's word; that will happen when we read it; we study it; we meditate upon it.* What a joy to know that we will indeed be changed as we read and study God's word. We do not need to strain, follow a list of man-made rituals or rules, fret, or become frustrated because we always come up short. We read, study, and meditate on the word. We are changed as we immerse ourselves in our Father's word to us and do all He bids us do; with His help- **Rest in that for a moment**.

Our services are indeed immersed from beginning to end with the Word of God. Verses are read continually throughout the service. This has become one of my favorite parts of our service. I love to hear the word as our pastor, and other appointed members, read scriptures. I love to see the scriptures on the screen. This has become a joy for me.

Praise

"Now may the God of hope fill you with all joy and peace in believing, that you may abound in hope by the power of the Holy Spirit." (Romans 15:13 KJV)

Praise You, Dear God that You are teaching me to enjoy every day of my life. You are causing me to walk in *all joy* and hope, by the *power of the Holy Spirit.*

"I will praise You, for I am fearfully and wonderfully made; marvelous are your

works, and that my soul knows very well."
(Psalms 139:14 KJV)

I praise You that I am fearfully and wonderfully made.

"For I know the plans I have for you, declares the Lord, Plans to prosper you and not to harm you, plans to give you hope and a future."
(Jeremiah 29:11 NIV)

I praise You that you have good plans for me; plans to give me a hope and a future.

A Daily Prayer

I have learned, and am still learning, that I cannot do anything apart from God. Only through leaning on Him can I have any success; from eating healthy to walking in joy and hope.

Out of the abundance of my constant need for God's help and my desire to walk in His will every day

of my life, evolved this heartfelt cry
of my heart- **My Daily Prayer and
Desire**

> ➢ **That every day might be
> a happy adventure, full of
> hope and wonder; even
> in the midst of sameness
> and necessary routines.**
> ➢ **That I might lean on You,
> Dear God, for all things.**
> ➢ **That I might walk in Your
> perfect will and plan for
> me every day with great
> joy, hope and
> expectation.**
> ➢ **That I might overcome all
> things and rejoice in You
> in the midst of all
> circumstances.**
> ➢ **That I might become as a
> little child in my faith,
> hoping, and trusting in
> God; totally at rest
> knowing My Heavenly
> Father cares for me, and
> is in control of all things.**

➢ **That I might delight, and rest in Your perfect will every day of my life.**
➢ **That I might think only good and right thoughts according to Philippians 4:8.**
➢ **That I might enjoy every day of my life.**
➢ **That I might choose, and not refuse, joy always. In Jesus' Name, Amen.**

We can pray, hope, and rejoice for God is indeed working a wonderful work in our life. According to Joyce Meyer, (The Everyday Life Bible; pg. 572; *The First Step to Fullness*) God brings us to a wonderful place of total dependence on Him- an empty vessel. Enjoy the journey dear friend and reader.

Additionally, always remember to take **one day at a time**. Pray every morning-
Dear God, today I choose joy in You. If there is anything hindering my joy today, please show me that I might overcome; and help me to overcome. I lean on You, for Your burden is light. It is a light thing to choose joy. In Jesus' Name, Amen. (Matthew 6:34)

Finally, when you find yourself in a situation, circumstance, or a trying time that you don't understand, go back to the last thing God instructed your heart to do, and do that.
Dear God, I don't understand this time. I am not sure how to respond to the trial before me. But I do know that You have instructed my heart to choose joy in all circumstances; to focus on You; that You are my constant help; and to lean on You to overcome all things. In Jesus' Name, Amen.

Cite Sources/Bibliography

1. Unless otherwise indicated, all scripture has been taken from the *King James Version (KJV)*.
2. Limited scripture reflects the *New Internation Version (NIV) @ Copyright 1973,1978, 1984 International Bible Society.* Used by permission. All rights reserved. Zondervan.
3. Some verses reflect the *New King James Version (NKJV). Copyright 1982 by Thomas Nelson, Inc. Used by permission. All rights reserved.* The text of the New King James Version (NKJV) may be quoted or reprinted without prior written permission with the following qualifications:
   a. Up to and including 1,000 verses may be quoted in print form as long as the verses quoted amount to less than 50% of the total work in which they are quoted;

b. All NKJV quotations must conform accurately to the NKJV text.
Any use of the NKJV text must include a proper acknowledgement as follows: Some scripture taken from the New King James Version. Copyright 1982 by Thomas Nelson, Inc.

4. Some scripture taken from the Amplified Bible, Copyright 1954,1958, 1964, 1965, 1987 by the Lockman Foundation.

5. Ten Boom, Corrie *with* Elizabeth and John Sherrill; *The Hiding Place*; Chosen Books. *Mi. 2006.*

6. Meyer, Joyce. *The Everyday Life Bible; The First Step to Fullness.* New York 2006. *Seven Things That Steal Your Joy: You Can Live a Life of Joy. New York. Time Warner Book Group. 2004.*

7. Stanley. Charles. *The Charles F. Stanley Life Principles Bible: What the Bible says about how*

to handle feelings of guilt.
(828) Charles Stanley. 2005.

8. Kirkpatrick. William J. *Lord I'm Coming Home. 1892*

9. Hall. Elvina M. *Jesus Paid it All. 1865.*

10. Smith. Laura. L. *Restore My Soul, The Power & Promise of 30 Psalms (quote)*

Happy God's Way

About the Author

Donnadene King lives in the beautiful hills of Kentucky with her husband Todd, two handsome boys (Jesse and Austin Hager); and a Cavachon named Floki.

Mrs. King has taught school in Kentucky and West Virginia for 24+ years. Her husband Todd is, also, an educator and writer. (Look for his books to be published soon. However, according to Mrs. King, she has no intention of reading his most excellent books as they are too creepy and too scary.)

Mrs. King's son, Jesse, used his research skills to collaborate with his mom on the book- searching out verses and exploring the legalities of citing sources. Jesse, Austin, and Mr. King served as proofreaders and advisors on the project.

Austin, also, used his skills (and degree in Music Production) to produce several videos for his mom's class. Videos can be found on YouTube- Donna King ABC or Donna King Vowels. Her husband created the graphics-farm scene.

Donnadene King

donnadeneking@gmail.com

www.ingramcontent.com/pod-product-compliance
Lightning Source LLC
LaVergne TN
LVHW051414080426
835508LV00022B/3074